HOW TO GIVE UP SHOPPING
SHOPPING
(or at least cut down)

For my sister, Victoria

Published in 2009
by Hardie Grant Books
85 High Street
Prahran, Victoria 3181, Australia
www.hardiegrant.com.au

Copyright text © Neradine Tisaj 2009
Copyright illustrations © Danie Pout 2009

A catalogue record for this book is available from the
National Library of Australia.
ISBN: 978 1 74066 735 7

Design and illustrations by Danie Pout
Cover photograph courtesy of Lara Burke at *Frankie* magazine
Typeset by Megan Ellis
Printed and bound in Australia by Griffin Press

· 10 9 8 7 6 5 4 3 2 1

HOW TO GIVE UP SHOPPING

(or at least cut down)

The journey back to conscious spending

NERADINE TISAJ

Hardie Grant Books

Contents

1

Introduction

My shopping story and why financial planners didn't understand me

21

Chapter One

Why do we over-shop?

37

Chapter Two

What's your shopping style? And yes, shopping for other people still counts

51

Chapter Three

The shopping detox – have you been in your cupboards lately?

67

Chapter Four

The boring stuff – build boundaries and learn to play the shopping game

79

Chapter Five

Sales are not your friend and credit cards are the devil's work

93

Chapter Six

Sorry, but you can't actually shop your way to inner happiness

105

Chapter Seven

Okay, here it is – the journey back to conscious spending

117

Conclusion

What does not kill us makes us stronger – or so they say …

Introduction

*My shopping story and why financial
planners didn't understand me*

Every year for as long as I can remember, I have had 'save money'
on my list of New Year's resolutions. When I was a teenager, I
spent all my money on clothes. While my friends had posters of
Duran Duran and Michael Jackson on their walls, I had posters
of *Vogue* covers. I plastered my school folders with images of
fashion models; I spent my pocket money on French and Italian
fashion magazines and made lists of clothes I aspired to buy.

I was totally obsessed with fashion and trends – it seemed to be the key to a special world I wanted to belong to. My sister, on the other hand, saved all her money and borrowed my clothes. After many volatile fights (the sort that only sisters have), my mother implemented a system: my sister had to pay me to borrow my clothes. She basically rented them. It stopped us fighting for a while, but it didn't change the scoresheet at the end of the day: she still managed to save most of her money and I still had a great wardrobe, but no savings.

More than twenty years later, not much has changed. The intrinsic issue is that I love clothes shopping, and my sister hates it. And so she still has more money than I do.

I am a shopper. I love shopping and I'm good at it. But after buying my first home I realised I needed to change my lifestyle. It seems that owning my own home and continuing to add to my fabulous collection of pink shoes wasn't very realistic. And credit card bills and a mortgage are not really great accessories to have in your life when interest rates are unpredictable. So I went to bookshops and picked up everything I could about personal finance. I read it all and still had no answers that applied to me. So I went for the personalised touch: after a series of depressing visits to financial planners, I realised I needed to cut down on my shopping, but no one could actually tell me *how*. How do you cut out something that makes you happy? What I did understand was that this was not going to be easy; it would take planning, discipline and a change of habits, similar to embracing a new healthy lifestyle.

Read any financial book and it will tell you to spend less and save more. Easier said than done. It's just like the weight loss book that tells you to eat less and exercise more – it's a simple equation and yet so many of us can't get it right. Every news report these days seems to have something about increasing obesity or consumer debt. We are getting fatter and so are our credit card bills.

I'm not a psychologist, a finance expert or a self-help guru. I'm just someone who managed to get her shopping habit under control (most of the time). And I understand the mindset of over-shoppers, so open up your Gucci wallet and empty out all those receipts, because in time you will be able to face your inner shopping demons, and make the journey back to conscious spending.

My shopping story

I started behind the pack and never quite caught up. My parents immigrated to Australia and built a great life for my sister and me.

But things went pear-shaped when their business was robbed and put into receivership. Long story short, my family lost everything. Then a film project my sister and I were working on fell through. For a while I felt like we were cursed. We got on with our lives eventually, but my relationship with money became a complicated one. Instead of becoming very careful with money, I became an over-shopper.

Apparently it's all about balance …

They say you can have it all, just not all at once. I don't really believe in balance. I think that if you are going to achieve something and be truly successful at it – whether it's bringing up children or having a career – you are going to have to make some sacrifices and lose some balance along the way. I don't think this has to be a bad thing; you just need to take time once in a while to reassess your life strategies along the way so that you don't lose perspective.

I worked for a TV network and was on call 24/7. My life revolved around television, so much so that I didn't realise I had become the clichéd female workaholic – single, renting and spending. And boy, did I spend. Shopping was one of my reliefs, one of the things that I felt made me happy. It didn't require any special equipment or organising phone calls; it was just me, the shopping mall and my credit cards, and I thought it was providing a release from my stressful life. Whenever I had a spare moment I would duck into a store and make a quick purchase. I got so good at it, I could even multi-task it – many a TV crisis was dealt with while I was on the phone in a department store changing room.

One weekend I was out with a friend who works as a meditation teacher. We were having a chat about all sorts of things – life, love, the pursuit of happiness – and she asked me what gave me joy in my life.

'My Prada handbag,' I replied. 'That gives me joy.'

She looked at me with a sympathy I didn't understand. I didn't realise how out of control my life had become.

I took a couple of weeks off from my crazy job and went to a retreat. There, in the enforced quiet, I realised that TV was not the most important thing in the world and that I needed to get a life outside of it. If I hadn't embraced this idea fully, it was driven home the weekend we launched a reality TV show. The show's stylist had called me at midnight because the host's Armani pants were missing and we had to work out how to find a new outfit. It was madness, but we managed to solve the crisis at the last minute. In the meantime, my father was in hospital recovering from a stroke. My family had decided not to tell me because I was away working on the launch. They didn't want to bother me.

I was devastated when I found out. My life was so out of balance – all my priorities were wrong. I wanted to run away from it all, but it was too late. By that stage I had a huge mortgage and massive credit card bills – running away was out of the question. And, despite all the stress, on many levels I still loved my job. I loved my staff and the people I worked with, I enjoyed the creativity and the interesting people, and I loved TV. But the pace was killing me.

I went to my mentor, an old-school TV exec, for advice. He said it was time to look for a new job and, as soon as I started looking, the universe presented me with one. A new job in TV, which allowed me to work in an industry I loved but didn't require that I be on call all the time. And so I started to get my life back in order.

My life admin was out of control – I'd kept shoving bills and papers in boxes, thinking I would have time to get to them one day, not to mention the wardrobe that caused me angst every time I opened it, or the bathroom drawers crammed with products I didn't use, and kitchen cupboards that spewed out Tupperware and pots every time I opened them. My apartment was bursting at the seams and yet I couldn't find anything I needed. This was only made worse by the fact that every time I came home I had more shopping bags.

Plus, now that I had weekends off, I was lost. I had no hobbies so I went out with friends, watched TV, read books, worked out at the gym and shopped. I shopped and shopped and shopped.

Why financial planners don't understand us

I knew my finances were out of control and so, like a yo-yo dieter, I went on an endless search for a magic solution. Friends often asked why I kept buying financial books and seeing financial planners and accountants. The answer was simple: I was on a quest.

I bought and read many financial books: *Think and Grow Rich*, *The Millionaire Next Door*, *The Richest Man in Babylon*, *The Science of Getting Rich*, *How to Get Rich*, *The 9 Steps to Financial Freedom*. They were all great and still sit on my bookshelf, and I understood the concept they were based on – save part of everything you earn and reinvest it. But I didn't understand *how* to save; the more I earned, the more I spent, which I've since learned is quite common. You get a pay rise so you go to a better restaurant and order a more expensive wine; you get a bonus so you buy a bigger TV; a bit more in the bank each month and your shoes go from Target to Manolo's – *that* concept made more sense to me than saving. I made budgets I never stuck to because it seemed that nothing made me feel better than buying some fab new shoes or fashion magazines or make-up.

After the finance guides, I bought all the books I could find on de-cluttering and organising your life. I felt energised but I still kept shopping; it had become part of who I was. But I didn't think it was a *problem*. I watched talk show after talk show, showing women who'd bought $5000 designer handbags and then hidden them in their wardrobes. I shook my head. *These* women had problems. I'd never hidden a handbag in my wardrobe – what, and miss the chance of actually using it? – so I didn't think I had a real issue. I used everything I bought (or so I thought) and, being single and living alone, there was no one to judge or comment on the number of shopping bags that accumulated each week. No one could point out what I couldn't see myself.

My credit card debt was growing and, because of my salary at this time, it was easy for me to get more credit (way too easy). Interest rates and fuel prices were rising and, like many other people who had been given home loans and credit cards, I was sinking into a debt vortex. I thought if I found the right financial planner, they would somehow find more money for me.

I must admit I've never responded well to tough love. I've dumped quite a few nazi-like personal trainers and nutritionists in favour of the warm, fuzzy variety. I need people to tell me that I am wonderful before they tell me what's wrong with me. Perhaps it's a reaction to my strict Catholic education, stern nuns and teachers who discouraged individualism and creativity. So when I started looking for a financial planner I wanted someone kind and supportive. Someone who would condone all the shopping I did, but would tell me something interesting and creative to do with my mortgage so that suddenly I would have more cash flow. *Sure you can keep on spending, but if you move your accounts around and do some clever things with your tax return, you'll be able to pay off all your debts, invest in some stocks and get rich.* Yeah, it took me a while to realise these mythical creatures didn't exist. I had a totally false impression of what financial planners actually did.

Since then, without being *too* dismissive, I've realised that financial planners are the gym junkies of the finance world. They just don't get that things might be hard for the rest of us poor souls. Just as gym junkies do back-to-back classes, live off protein shakes and can only talk about working out, financial planners obsess over numbers, saving money and investing it. They don't get people who earn money but can't seem to keep hold of it. Okay, so I'm a bit bitter, but I have had three bad experiences with financial planners, and, as with bad boyfriends, I was starting to wonder if *I* was the one with the problem. And of course I was.

Eventually, I had the epiphany: they just don't understand shoppers or, in my case, over-shoppers. A financial planner telling an over-shopper to simply save more money by cutting down on spending was like a marathon runner telling an obese person to just get off the sofa and exercise more. It was never going to work until I understood what I was doing and why. Still, off I went into

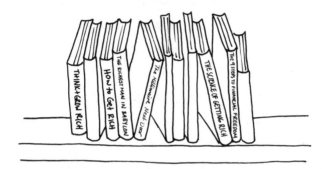

the world of financial planners looking for a magic cure, like the woman who wants to lose those extra few pounds but still wants doughnuts for breakfast. I was delusional; I just didn't know it.

The slick financial planner

The first financial planner I went to was recommended by a friend with a lot of money. In fact, I think this was the only reason he agreed to see me – my friend was an important celebrity client. I was working as a TV publicist at the time and had come from a hectic photo shoot with brattish wannabe popstars. I was exhausted. I'd started work at 6 am and had had too much coffee and chocolate, as one does on these shoots, which probably made me appear even more neurotic than usual.

The financial planner's office was slick, with a breathtaking view of Sydney Harbour. I sat down in the waiting room, holding a pile of ragged pages – financial notes I'd scrawled on some available paper at the photo shoot. His receptionist could have been a model, with perfect hair and nails and a general air that makes regular people feel scruffy. Already, I felt compelled to go out and buy new clothes and shoes.

The financial planner swept out and was civil but condescending, and I immediately regressed to an insecure teenager. In the time it took to enter his office, I became that girl with braces and pimples at dance class, surrounded by boys who also had braces and pimples as well as sweating palms and the mingled scent of Clearasil and Brut 33. I noticed I had a hole in my stockings as I sat down.

'So you're a friend of so and so's.' He looked me up and down. I obviously wasn't the A-list client he was expecting. He asked what my annual income was and, after choking slightly when I told him, he then kind of squirmed when I gave him my hand-written financial notes. He scanned them for a minute or two and then handed them back. 'I'm sorry, but you actually need to *have* some money before I can tell you what to do with it.'

'Oh.' I looked back down at my notes. 'To be honest, I don't really know where my money goes. I thought I was on quite a good salary for my age.'

'Don't worry, I have clients who earn a million dollars a year and still don't have any savings, or any idea of where their money goes.'

This was some consolation, but not particularly helpful. I decided my situation wasn't that bad. I stuffed my crumpled papers into my over-priced designer handbag, went on my way, and kept shopping.

I found the experience more humiliating than I can explain, so it was a while before I could sum up the courage to venture into this territory again. For some reason, talking about money and my own financial situation made me feel like I had stripped down and asked a stranger to critique my body. I know it sounds ridiculous but that's how I felt then and it hasn't changed. Even more ridiculous was that I had studied economics at university and had managed million-dollar budgets in many of my jobs – I prided myself on always coming in just under budget on work projects – and yet my personal finances were a disaster. It didn't make sense. Every month on pay day, I'd feel rich and go splurge – I call it drunken sailor mentality – and then that last week of the month I was always scrounging around in handbags, coat pockets and secret hiding places for small change. The thought of trying to explain it to another financial planner was too much. But I still hoped for that mythical planner who could help …

The frumpy financial planner

The second financial planner was the subject of dinner-party stories for the next few months. She was the same age as me (late thirties, shall we say), but she dressed like she was twenty years older, had terrible hair and bad shoes and spoke to me in the tone of the teachers who taught me at school – condescending and punishing. We were destined never to bond, something I felt was important for some reason. Not that I expected that she would become my new best friend or that we would go out for cocktails, but surely you were meant to bond with, and like, your financial advisor?

This time I'd typed up my financial statements to seem like I was more in control of my finances and my life. It didn't really help. She told me I needed to save some money before she could tell me what to do with it. Again, it was all about if I ever had money – only then could they tell me what to do with it. I was hoping she would give me some advice about how to structure my mortgage or if there were any ways to minimise my tax or other such helpful tips to increase my income.

Her advice?

'You need to stop spending money on clothes and getting your hair done.'

I have blonde highlights – they are not negotiable.

'Also, it would be much easier if you had a husband to share your mortgage repayments with.'

Oh *really*. She wasn't alone in that thought – I'd bought a popular book on paying off your mortgage in a few years only to find it was based on the premise that a couple lives off one person's wage and saves the other. I wish I could get my money back on that one. If you are a single woman with a mortgage, the advice seems to be to get a husband – we haven't really come that far, have we?

I was starting to feel like a character in a Jane Austen novel, with no dowry and the need to be married off to avoid life as a poor spinster. I told the advisor that the 'getting a husband' option was not going to help me in the short term, and anyway I had more romantic notions about why people got married.

'Can you give me any advice about where you think I should cut back on my spending?' I asked.

She looked at my list of expenses. 'You should probably give up sponsoring the three World Vision children – that's excessive. Couldn't you just have one?'

Now, after a Catholic education and years of watching *Oprah*, I knew that wasn't the right thing to do, and it would definitely give me even worse financial karma than I already had, not to mention terrible guilt.

'Anything else?' I asked.

'Well, you spend far too much money on going out.' (I had been quite honest in the budget I'd given her.) 'You should stay at home more and not get take-out. You know, you can do a lot of creative things with a dozen eggs.'

I tried to compose myself. 'I'm a single woman living in Sydney. I work long hours. I can't stay at home on my own eating eggs – I'd become suicidal.'

She looked at me squarely and said, 'Well, if you want to save some money, you'll have to. How much was that?' She pointed to the box of sushi I had brought with me. 'You really should be making your own lunch.'

There was an awkward pause.

'Are you okay? You look depressed.'

I left her office deflated, haunted by images of sitting at home alone every weekend eating boiled eggs while attempting to do my own highlights with disastrous results (one bad home-dye job is enough to scar a girl for life). Soon after, I got a new credit card and went out on a month-long spending spree. My friends still make jokes about me staying at home and eating eggs.

The financial planner who said I was beyond help
This time it was a friend – an ex-banker and a financial planner. I thought she would be kinder, but because she was a friend she

just let loose. She's one of those people who have been investing in property since their first job, and not coincidentally she hated clothes shopping. She can never understand why people don't have money, she has always paid her credit cards on time and only spends money she has.

She looked at my numbers and told me to move out of my apartment and rent something smaller, so I could get a better tax break. But I loved my apartment. After years and years of renting, it was such a relief to live somewhere that felt like home – a feeling I hadn't experienced since my family lost ours. So this time, I decided I would take matters into my own hands. I would simply figure out a way to save more and shop less.

There seems to be two extremes when it comes to financial guidance: help for people who are in debt crisis or living in poverty, and financial planners for people who have a great deal of money and want to know how to make more. For those of us in between there isn't much out there. So this book is not for everybody; it's for us over-shoppers. Shopping itself is not bad; it's over-shopping and getting into debt that is. Take back your power – don't be a credit card or debt victim. Make the journey back to conscious spending and decide what is important to you.

Chapter One

Why do we over-shop?

It's hard to give up something you are good at – just watch any ageing popstar talk about the glory days and you'll see that hint of sadness in their eyes – so if shopping has become your hobby, something you are *fabulous* at, then it will be something incredibly difficult to let go of.

I definitely treated shopping as a hobby, something I did to relax. It started in my early twenties, while I was living in New York City. The city really shaped my value system – young New Yorkers live in tiny shoebox apartments so they spend all their money on going out and looking good. There's no point in buying things for your apartment when you and your futon can barely fit in it, and the idea of owning your own home is as far-fetched as being a rockstar. And so we shopped. It wasn't extravagant, but my friends and I would spend days browsing the amazing department stores and boutiques of New York. Most of what we actually bought was inexpensive – clothes from sample sales and thrift stores, second-hand books and jewellery from flea markets. We looked out for sale time and became friends with the shop assistants, who would tell us when to find the best bargains.

When I came back to Australia, shopping was ingrained as something to do to relax – it was like walking around art galleries or museums. I loved department stores the best. I loved that one minute you could be trying on a hat, then the next minute there'd be some shoes, and a few steps away a new perfume, then up an escalator an evening gown, down another escalator a juicer and some bed sheets. Yes, I think heaven is a great big department store. It helped that, as a child, a trip to the department store was a day's excursion away from dull suburbia and into the wonderful world of the city.

But the truth is, it's not just department stores. I love all shops and stores – I love pharmacies, fruit and vegetable shops, hardware stores, bookstores and delis. I love seeing all the products laid out with lots of choice; I like making the decisions about what to buy. It gives me a sense of purpose; I must have been a descendant of some hunter/gatherer types (likely I was the Queen of the Gatherers), but what was picking wild berries was now buying beautiful shoes that I could barely walk in.

People often suggested I pursue a career in personal shopping. It never interested me – I didn't want it to become a job because I loved it too much. Instead, it became a habit – I shopped to treat myself when I was bored, stressed, tired, grumpy, feeling unappreciated, I shopped when I had put on weight and when I was angry. But I also shopped to celebrate, when I was happy with something I had accomplished, when I was in love, when I was feeling good about myself, when I was on holiday, when I was working – it was one of the only ways I knew to nurture myself.

I thought I was just like Holly Golightly in *Breakfast at Tiffany's*. Just as she only felt safe in the jewellery store Tiffany's, so I looked for solace in shopping. I saw that film for the first time on television when I was ten years old. I taped it and watched it over and over again throughout my teens. I guess it's no great surprise that it's one of my favourite films – what woman doesn't want a present from Tiffany's, all boxed up in beautiful blue and tied with white satin ribbon? – but it could have been any number of other movies. The fairytale of retail therapy has always been part of Hollywood.

That scene in *Pretty Woman* where Julia Roberts returns from a successful shopping trip, armed with paper bags? We all love it. After a bad initial experience, she deserves her triumph; the fact that she's a hooker using a client's credit card to achieve it doesn't seem to bother any of us. If anything, it underlines just how much shopping can change a person – can *better* a person. We love a movie makeover – the new clothes, shoes, handbags, jewellery –

isn't it the Cinderella story being repeated over and over again? Someone coming to transform us from the ordinary woman we think we are to the immediately more attractive woman, complete with a busty evening dress and ridiculously high shoes. Years later, programs like *Sex and the City* showed us that we didn't even need to rely on a man to make us over; we could do it ourselves, so the fairytale continued. And I for one embraced it wholeheartedly.

The rise of the celebrity hasn't helped either. Years ago, movie stars lived in a world that was an inaccessible fantasy land. Grace Kelly and Audrey Hepburn swanned around at awards and events, but we didn't see them buying groceries at the supermarket or caught without make-up. Photos were staged for magazines – on the red carpet or at home photo shoots, which were styled perfectly – their lives looked like the glamorous movies they starred in; they did not seem like lives anywhere close to ours.

Now we see celebrities living the same lives we do – they grab take-out coffees and walk their dogs, they have big nights out on the town and have wardrobe malfunctions – and it looks like with a little effort, maybe if we had the right accessories, we could be as fabulous as they seem. But they don't *really* live the same lives. Just because they share some of the same pastimes doesn't mean we should judge ourselves by what we perceive to be their standards.

These people have a great deal more money than you and I, and should not be used as role models. We cannot emulate their lives and shouldn't try. They have personal trainers, personal chefs, nannies and a host of other people supporting their lifestyles – we, on the other hand, are doing it on our own. I've worked with celebrity mothers who bang on about how hard it is to have a career and be a mother – all the while making it look simple and elegant – but they never reveal that they have a cottage industry at home of three nannies on 24-hour rotation, personal assistants, housekeepers and chefs. Their lives are worlds away from ours, so stop comparing.

Oh, and their glorious wardrobes? Their effortless style? Most of what they wear has been given to them; it is often part of their job. They haven't blown their monthly budgets on a pair of sunglasses or a leather jacket, so they can afford to smile when they're caught on camera. Don't get me wrong, I don't dislike or resent celebrities, I just know that the reality of their lives is quite different from ours, and I find myself constantly reminding friends who envy the hair, body, home and wardrobe of certain celebrities that they shouldn't make those comparisons and beat themselves up about their own flaws. These celebs have all the same problems with family and personal relationships that we do, and all the same insecurities and fears. Just because you have your hair and make-up done every morning before you walk out the door to your chauffeur-driven limo doesn't necessarily mean your husband is going to be faithful or your children will behave. It probably just means that you will be photographed even more when you are falling apart than when your life is together. If anything, you should feel sorry for celebrities. So if you over-shop to meet the standards that celebrities set, next time you see your fave celeb photographed with that Hermès handbag you crave, remember they are probably even more strung-out about life than you are. And that the handbag will make you no happier than it made them.

We can't blame *all* our problems on a celebrity-obsessed society, sadly. So why *do* we over-shop? Probably for the same reasons we over-indulge in food and alcohol, smoke cigarettes, gamble, over-exercise – stress, boredom and emotional worry. But I think it mainly has to do with filling the void. What do I mean by the void? Well, I guess not everyone feels it, but for me it's that niggling feeling that something is missing in your life, that you are not doing things quite right – an existential insecurity about why you are here and what your purpose is in life.

Modern life has put extra pressure on us: we have less support from our family and communities, we are busy trying to do too much and we lose awareness of who we are and what really makes us happy. So we try to fill the void with quick fixes. But, as you have probably already noticed, the quick fixes don't really work. That new pair of earrings is not going to cover up the fact that you hate your job or that your best friend has stopped talking to you. It's not going to make you feel any more purposeful about life.

Shopping is neither the answer to all the big spiritual questions of the world nor the thing to do just to fill time. So many of us treat it as a habit or a hobby, but we really shouldn't – that's not what it is supposed to be. Shopping is meant to be what you do when you need something. It was never supposed to be an emotional crutch. So learn to change your shopping habits: if you really need something, you should only go to that particular store, purchase that one thing and go home. If you can, don't take your wallet, just take your driver's licence and the cash you need to make your purchase, so you're not tempted. It will feel like you're missing something, but it does protect you from over-spending.

Even though we might use it as a weird form of relaxation, shopping can actually cause stress, especially if you are buying on credit, because even if you are getting a little hit when you make

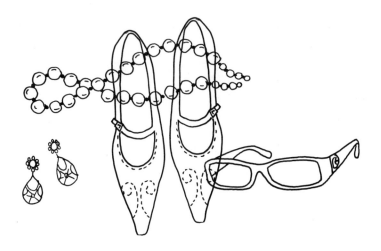

your purchase, you are also probably feeling stressed and guilty at a subconscious level. Have you noticed the looks people have on their faces when they're at a shopping mall? They don't look particularly happy; they usually look stressed, especially when you compare the looks on people's faces when they're in a park, beach, museum, gallery, church or fete/fair/festival/concert. People in shopping malls are not really having fun – are they? They usually look dazed and confused, or stressed, rushed and haggard.

A hobby is something that should occupy *and* enrich you, and it should do so without giving you heart palpitations (apparently shoppers get the same rush gamblers do). If you are an over-shopper, like me, you will have to ditch shopping as your hobby, and go out and find a new one. This isn't as easy as it sounds; it will be a process of elimination.

I've always thought of hobbies as something quite lame, something that boring people do. I was of the 'work hard, play hard' school. I'd never been into arts and crafts and the only clubs I'd ever belonged to were nightclubs. Of course, this was a recipe for burnout, but I had to discover it the hard way, on a number of occasions. As I'd always been quite ambitious, I only wanted to do things that promoted my career. I didn't see the point of sitting in a chair, knitting – it wasn't social and it wasn't helping me up the ladder. Of course, I've since changed my mind.

When I was at my most stressed-out, an executive coach recommended I read *Flow* by Mihaly Csikszentmihalyi. Its basic premise is that people find happiness when they are doing activities in which they are so immersed that they don't notice time passing or the need for food, and they lose their sense of ego. Everyone has something that makes them feel like this, but as we get older we lose track of them so it's good to remind yourself. Think about the things you enjoyed doing as a child or teenager, things you got totally lost in. Athletes often refer to the feeling as being 'in the zone', musicians as being 'in the groove' and artists as being inspired or hearing their 'muse'. Think about what this is for you. You might need to try a few things to find out – don't worry if you make a few mistakes along the way, it's all part of your journey.

For me, it was cutting out recipes from magazines and newspapers and pasting them into a book. I love doing this in front of a favourite TV show or old movie, and I can do it for hours. Of course, this isn't a hobby you want to talk about at dinner parties, and you're probably already rolling your eyes and thinking how boring it sounds. I must have been thinking this myself on some level as I went out to find other, more impressive hobbies.

First I learned golf. Initially it was to play with my father for his seventieth birthday, but I discovered I quite enjoyed it. It didn't hurt that a very charming golf pro was there to encourage me. I convinced two friends to learn with me; they also found the golf pro very charming. And now we play once a month at a hokey public course and always have fun. Golf also works as therapy – I've found that going to the driving range when you're angry with the world and hitting a bucket of balls is a great release, and much cheaper than buying a pair of designer shoes. You do need to be careful, though, that your new hobby doesn't become an excuse to

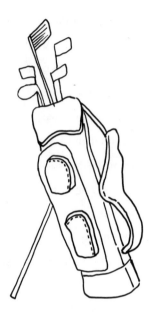

shop more. It would have been easy to get carried away spending money on golf paraphernalia (although women's golfing outfits are pretty hideous), but instead I took a deep breath and bought a set of second-hand clubs on eBay.

Golf was fun but I needed more distractions. Next, I enrolled in an ocean swimming class and trained for a race, which scared the hell out of me – like many Australians, I grew up with a fear of sharks. I trained twice a week, and when I swam in the rough surf during a thunderstorm at six o'clock in the morning, I thought

I must be losing my mind. But when I eventually swam the race and raised money for a charity while doing it, I was filled with a real sense of achievement. This was something *I* created, something *I* accomplished, without anything to bite me in the bum later. The glory didn't come with the sting of shame or guilt, it was all just glory. Shopping could never give me this. I still hate getting up in the early morning and I still hate cold water, but I'm quite confident about swimming in the ocean now. I'm very slow (I blame my short arms) but I do it when I can and I love it.

Inspired by the swimming, I decided maybe I was a sporty person after all, so I began training for a half-marathon – yeah, right. I hate running, always have, but I decided that completing a half-marathon sounded very impressive. But I wasn't being true to myself – I was trying to be tough because at the time I was feeling lost in my career path. The running training was some sort of way of dealing with it. Anyway, after a 14-kilometre training run, from which I sustained blisters in places one should never have blisters, I realised running was not for me. At the time, I felt like a bit of a quitter, but I'm okay about it now and I continue to explore new things that don't involve shopping or even spending money.

I should note that finding a new hobby may not cut it for everyone. I've read a lot about a new disorder that Stanford University doctors have identified as 'obsessive shopping disorder'. There are all these stories on the Internet about people who are obsessive about their shopping – like the man in the US who kept buying wrenches (at last count he had more than 2000). This is not what I consider 'over-shopping'; this is a more serious affliction. If you feel like your shopping is an addiction and it's really affecting the quality of your life, you probably need to think about seeing a psychiatrist who deals with addiction. Debtors Anonymous also has meetings in most cities around the world, as well as providing a lot of information online which can help you assess whether you have an addiction issue. It appears that many people with addictions have shopping addictions, or develop them when they are recovering from another addiction.

For the rest of you, though – try finding a new hobby.

Tips to remember

- Only go shopping when you have something specific that you really need to purchase, and then only go to the relevant store to buy it.

- Don't browse.

- Don't shop when you are tired, stressed, emotional or under the influence of hormones.

- Don't go to a shopping mall because you have nothing else to do.

- Find a hobby, try a few things. It might take a while to find something you enjoy.

- If you think your over-shopping might be turning into an addiction, seek professional help from a psychiatrist; your local doctor can refer you to someone. Debtors Anonymous websites can be helpful in assessing if you have an addiction.

Chapter Two

*What's your shopping style? And yes,
shopping for other people still counts*

What is your shopping style? Do you buy high-end expensive items or lots of little bits and pieces? Do you buy things for yourself or for your children, partner or friends? Spend some time thinking about what you buy so that you can be conscious of whether it's working for you and how you can control it.

A good way to really see your style is to write down your recent purchases. Grab your old receipts and credit card statements.

Write down everything you've bought. Was there nothing for a while and then a binge shop? Or was it more constant, with smaller amounts of money spent on little comfort items? Have a look for any spending spikes and think back to how you felt around that time or if there was anything to prompt the outbreak. Keep recording your purchases for a while and you'll start to pick up on any patterns.

I tend to buy bits and pieces when I'm bored, stressed or frustrated at work. But when I'm nervous about a big event, insecure about a social engagement or working overseas, I get carried away and buy something extravagant. I have a wardrobe full of expensive evening wear that I am not quite ready to part with but may never wear again. Now that I know my patterns, I try to occupy myself with something else when I'm stressed. I can pinpoint the times when I'm likely to reach for a credit card, times when the shopping is more about emotion than need. And then I can redirect myself.

You might be a shopping 'grazer', buying things every day – often small items – just to pass the time and make things interesting. Shopping in this way may not be to counter those huge mood swings, but just something to keep your energy up. Grazers often don't even realise they're over-shoppers, because

the individual receipts aren't that large. A new handcream, a bra, a few magazines, a lip gloss – before you know it, a Saturday morning browse has cost you $200 and it hasn't even quenched your shopping thirst.

My sister tells me that bored or frustrated mothers are big grazers. A rainy day with kids plus a mall equals lots of shopping. Having to entertain small children alone when they can't go out and play will drive any sane woman to purchase impractical homewares and 800-thread-count cotton sheets in order to feel better. Grazers would do well to adopt the 'take cash and driver's licence only' method, when you know you will be in the vicinity of stores and feeling vulnerable.

You might be a 'special occasions' shopper, 'treating' yourself to something every so often – you work hard, you deserve it. Or at least, you *thought* it was every so often. It might be closer to just 'often'. Your receipts won't lie, so be honest with yourself and your shopping rituals.

Think about how you feel when you want to buy something. What is the underlying motivation? If you can start to understand how and why you shop, you will be able to make some adjustments to your over-shopping habits. You may still need to shop but at least you can do it wisely. A friend of mine works in the music industry, and in her job she needs to stay on top of fashion and trends. There's no way she can avoid shopping, so she buys cheaper clothes of the moment, wears them for a few months and then sells them on eBay or at flea markets. She's figured out the system that works for her. Another friend works in the arts, and prefers classic, more expensive pieces of clothing. Rather than spending a fortune more frequently, she has discovered a system that will meet her style requirements without killing the budget. She gets to travel to Europe once a year for her job, so she saves up and does all her clothes shopping overseas.

How do *you* shop for clothes? Do you buy everything the same way? Think about your personal style and try to stick to that in a way that works with how much money you have coming in. If you eat toast every morning, isn't it better to buy a great toaster than to spend hundreds of dollars on a bread-making machine that you never use? Shopping is personal, like relationships; only *you* know how you feel and think – don't let other people dictate your shopping style. Just try to figure out what works best for you. Some expensive things last and are worth the investment, whereas cheaper things fall apart quickly – look at the things in your home and wardrobe and see what you still enjoy and appreciate.

When I gave up shopping and went on my shopping detox (more of that in Chapter Three), I noticed I missed buying books more than anything else. So now I allow myself a book budget – I have a jar where I put my book money. Sometimes I don't buy anything for a while and sometimes I buy a second-hand book, but when I do buy a book, it's with my own money and in cash. It means I don't feel guilty and I can enjoy the purchase. Think about what you really love buying and see if you can set up a similar system. It's not unlike going on a diet and giving yourself a treat from time to time – it keeps you motivated. If you know you have something to look forward to you are more likely to stay on track. If you abstain totally (after the initial detox) you are bound to have a binge at some point.

One shopping style that doesn't immediately stand out as an over-shopping problem is the 'gifter'. You know the sort – constantly leaving little presents on doorsteps for birthdays, anniversaries, thank-yous, condolences, births, bon voyages or welcome backs. Any occasion is ripe for a little something special. And it doesn't feel like a guilty pastime if you're buying things for someone else …

A life coach pointed out to m
gifts usually reflected that the buye
themselves or the relationship they
This made me think before I bough
made me realise I became a little

gifts with someone and received something that wasn't near
expensive as the gift I'd given – this is not at all in the spirit of
giving and made me feel uncomfortable that I was thinking in
such a petty way. I now try to be considerate and thoughtful,
rather than extravagant. I also try to remind myself that the
things I treasure most are usually the things with emotional value
attached to them (although I do really love my super-high red and
pink Marc by Marc Jacobs heels).

Getting yourself into debt to buy gifts for other people does
not make sense. And there's something a little bit karmic about
it too. Creating stress for yourself to give someone a gift that you
can't afford is, in a way, transferring your stress to that person. If
you receive a gift that you know the giver can't afford, you generally
feel guilty. I know my grandmother was always very extravagant
with her grandchildren, and as I got older I felt terrible about
how much money she spent on us. Think about this in reverse: if
you are giving someone something you really can't afford, are you

n some of your stress or even resentment? It may sound
ut there, but it is definitely something to consider – give
s you can afford.

Last year a friend who was mortgaged to her eyeballs (like
many of us) and had two small children baked shortbread for all
her friends and family. She simply told everyone that that was
all she could afford to give that Christmas – it was a genuine gift
from the heart and came with warmth and kindness, and it was
appreciated and understood by everyone. It's not cool or trendy,
but simple gifts like these are still gifts and we need to shift our
mindsets about what is important when we give and receive. I'm
not suggesting that you start knitting jumpers for all your friends'
birthdays, but take your gifts back to the root of giving and away
from the sale catalogues you get in the mail.

People also remember a small act of kindness. I believe in
doing these for people you know – I know that random acts of
kindness towards strangers are in vogue, but I feel a bit weird
about paying the toll for the car behind me, which lots of self-
help books espouse. Being kind to people I know makes more
sense and is more rewarding, as is charity work. Kind acts could
include picking up a friend or family member from the airport –
it's nice to have someone waiting for you in the gate lounge;

taking someone fresh fruit or soup when they are sick; helping someone move house, or bringing them food when they have just moved in; offering to babysit someone's children for a night or looking after the neighbours' pets. These are things that most people forget to do, but they can have a lot more impact than a bought gift. They help build friendships and can create a sense of community.

I experienced a beautiful act of kindness years ago, which I always treasure. I had been going through a particularly difficult time: my mother was very sick in hospital, I was between jobs and my family was dealing with a stressful court case. Out for dinner one night, my friends took my wallet while I was in the bathroom and they all put some cash in it (ten of them put in $20 each). They didn't tell me and in my stressful state I never noticed that there was an extra $200 in my wallet, but I was grateful that I seemed to have more money than I thought. They told me years later, and I have since done similar things for other people.

If an occasion does require a gift, think about small, simple gifts. Have you ever noticed that children can get as excited over a tiny gift as they do over something huge? Their attention span is so short that for them it's the moment of receiving that has the most impact. I have a gift drawer at home where I keep

little things for children and a few generic gifts to take when the
occasion arises – DVDs, CDs, books and chocolates. Often when
you buy something at the last minute you feel pressured and end
up spending more than you'd intended to.

Gift substitutes can be tiny. I'm big on the handwritten note;
it's old-fashioned but so lovely to receive something in the mail
that's not a bill. I recently came across a suitcase full of postcards
from the 1960s at an antique store; they were twenty cents each
and I bought a stack to send as thank-you notes when someone
has done me a favour or had me over for dinner, or if I just want
to let someone know they are in my thoughts. I must admit that

I have baffled a few people: when they receive a postcard with a photo of Rome, circa 1968, saying thanks for dinner last week, they usually email back wondering where the hell I am.

I'll often send an article from a newspaper or magazine. It does take time, but I have a pigeon-hole in my home office where I put all these articles and, once every few weeks, I sit down and collect everything to send with a note – people are always so grateful. And, on a selfish note, it makes me feel good and connected to people in a way that gift-giving, emailing or texting does not.

Tips to remember

- Work out what you spend money on and how you are feeling when you do.

- Become aware of your weak moments.

- Buying things for other people can still result in over-shopping.

- It's a cliché, but when it comes to gifts, it is the thought that counts.

- Kind acts can be even more generous than giving gifts to family and friends.

- Work out the one thing that you enjoy buying the most and allow a budget for it. Only buy these items with cash that you have saved; do not buy it on credit card – make it a guilt-free, happy purchase.

Chapter Three

The shopping detox – have you been in
your cupboards lately?

In a new, less stressful job with weekends off, I suddenly had time to examine my life, and ironically it was really stressing me out. I went to see a life coach to sort myself out – she was great and helped to break my life into goals and small steps. She was incredibly supportive but she couldn't help but laugh when I told her one day that I'd discovered two identical blouses in my wardrobe. It seems I had bought the second one on a business trip.

I'd been looking after Chris Noth, who played Mr Big on *Sex and the City*. He was fond of cigars and, after spending a week with him on tour, all my clothes reeked of smoke. Chris was booked to appear on a talk show, and I'd heard that the Foo Fighters would be in the green room. Like an awestruck adolescent, I ran out to buy a new top – I wanted to look, and feel, good. (You should know that the job is not half as glamorous as it may sound – ask any publicist and they will tell you they feel more like a slave/nanny/bodyguard a great deal of the time – but I digress.) Now this wasn't a plain white T-shirt that I had bought twice; it was a frilly, black organza blouse from a well-known designer label – not an easy mistake to make. And yeah, I did end up meeting Dave Grohl but I very much doubt he remembers me or my top. But somehow it felt like a really important purchase at the time.

This amused my life coach to no end, and she asked if she could use it as an example for other clients. I obliged, but it made me feel sad at how busy and unconscious I must have been in my previous life to make such a mistake. To this day, I still have no recollection of when I bought the first shirt. Later, when I finally sorted out my apartment, I also found two copies of certain books and CDs and multiples of skincare and make-up products. It made me realise that I had lost a sense of myself – I'd existed with a lack of consciousness. I had been great at my job – I was totally dedicated to it – but I hadn't left any room for myself. At least, not enough room to know what I did or didn't have in my own home.

I know I'm not alone – friends tell me about duplicated groceries, shoes, track pants, baby clothes and moisturisers, bought with no memory of the one that already sat at home. So before you embark on your grand shopping cutback, you'll need to look at what you already have, and what you really need. This way, you'll have a clean, solid foundation for your new life.

It's time for your shopping detox.

Do you remember the last time you moved house? Did you think you had a lot more stuff than you realised and wondered where it had all come from? It's not an enjoyable experience, exactly – it usually makes you vow never to move again – but it would probably be good for over-shoppers to move every few years, because when you start going through all your things, you can see that you have too much. This is a great way to start your shopping detox, but you don't have to move house to take advantage of it – you can just pretend that you're about to move. Either way, you still need to organise and get rid of things.

So what is a shopping detox? Just like on a food detox, you'll need to give up some treats to get yourself back on track. It's

about taking stock of what you have and what you don't need. There are many books and heaps of websites about de-cluttering, sorting and organising your stuff – have a look at a few to see what you can relate to. This is my version but you'll work out what suits you, through trial and error.

There are two ways to start your shopping detox – the first step of your journey back to conscious spending. The first way is to write down everything you buy, so you can see what you are spending your money on. It's like the dreaded food diary. Get a notebook and draw up columns – date, time, store, item, price and how you were feeling when you made the purchase. Then record everything you buy and fill in each column. It can be slightly unnerving to see yourself go from purchasing a fresh juice and organic vegetables on a Monday to chocolate bars on Wednesday and then patent red heels on Thursday, after a bad day at the office or a rainy day at home with the kids.

The second method is to just go cold turkey – give up shopping and write down when you feel like buying something. I've tried the first way many times, but this was not as effective as when I just stopped shopping altogether. Besides, there is no way around it: you have to decide to give up shopping at some point, for a week, two weeks, a month, three months – whatever you decide is possible for you, it's individual. But it's the only way to get yourself back in balance and to stop over-shopping.

Give it up

When I say 'give up shopping', I mean stop buying anything that is not essential. But how do you define what is essential? Well, literally anything you cannot survive without – in the short term this usually just means food and fuel. There are communities around the world who only buy food, underwear and socks new, and everything else they buy second-hand. Other people have chosen not to spend money on anything but food (some even growing food); others are just against accruing stuff, so they allow themselves experiences, such as going to the movies or having massages. There are many books and stories on the Internet about these different groups, which can be inspiring, but they also tend to be a bit on the extreme side so don't let them freak you out. Sometimes it's just good to observe how other people get by.

Interestingly, the studies on longevity and health in communities in Japan, Italy and Russia, where it's not uncommon to live to over a hundred years old, show that these are also places where people live quite frugally with few modern devices. The ones who live the longest aren't the ones flashing their platinum credit cards or travelling the world with their Louis Vuitton luggage, they're the ones calmly drinking tea, contemplating life on a mountain top after their morning tai chi. Now, I'm not suggesting that you go all monastic or anything – I will *not* be shouting the virtues of staying home and eating boiled eggs anytime soon – but in your detox, it is important to strip it all back and get perspective. I think we have forgotten how simply we can live and still be happy and healthy.

Set aside a time when you will only shop for food (obviously you will have the usual living expenses – transport, household bills – so this doesn't count as shopping) and see how you feel. See what you miss most. Then, examine whether this is something that is truly important to you, something you may want to reintroduce into your life. But be careful. In the first few weeks I found myself transferring my over-shopping to food. The first time I didn't realise I had done it until I got to the supermarket checkout and the total was triple what I would normally spend. At the time I was too embarrassed to put anything back, so I paid for it and went home with all sorts of things I didn't need – designer jams, organic bubble bath, new fry pans.

The second time I did this, I realised before I got to the checkout and started putting things back. It was all a bit overwhelming – I ended up leaving the trolley and walking out of the supermarket (sorry to the person who had to reshelve everything). I felt ridiculous, but it ended up being a turning point. I knew that somewhere in my mind I must have thought that having these things would help me feel better about the stress in my life. I was a bit teary when I drove home to a house without food, but I knew I had done the right thing – I had started to break my over-shopping cycle.

And so merely going to the supermarket became a challenge. I used a basket instead of a trolley, even though it was always heavy, as it gave me an enforced limit. Obviously people with big families can't do this, so shopping online might help – you can set yourself a limit and continue to go back and return items easily. But remember: shopping online is still shopping.

It might take some time to get the grocery shopping down pat. After several weeks I still found myself walking around putting things back on shelves and doing a final check at the counter. Even then I would tell the checkout person if I didn't want something anymore. I'm sure the supermarket staff must have thought I had some sort of obsessive-compulsive disorder, but eventually my supermarket shopping became normal and I felt like I'd made a breakthrough, as silly as that might sound to someone without over-shopping issues.

Be careful not to double up on your detoxes, though. I decided to go on a big get fit and healthy campaign at the same time as I gave up shopping. I stopped going out, because I didn't want to eat or drink out, and I couldn't shop – all I allowed myself to do was go to the gym. Suffice to say, after a month of carrots and tofu, endless hours on treadmills, and staying home to avoid all shopping/eating/drinking temptations, I was practically suicidal.

I now definitely subscribe to the idea of getting one area of your life under control at a time. Don't expect too much of yourself, because it's going to take a while to get it all under control. And you are going to trip up along the way – trying to be perfect is boring and will only cause you grief, and multi-tasking your life is not always the right approach. Take one thing at a time, and slowly but surely other areas will fall into place.

Get rid of your crap

Your next step is to go forth into your cupboards and discover a world you had forgotten existed. Start slowly. Give yourself certain cupboards, rooms, areas, even drawers to sort through.

Eventually you will become a sorting machine. Put some good music on or ask someone to come round and chat while you do it – I'm told getting rid of the husband and children for the day can assist too – whatever helps. Again, there are books on exactly how to organise your house, but I find it helps if you can devise a system yourself – it will feel more empowering and, like exercise and diets, different things work for different people. For me, it was a reward system: I love sorting my books and shoes (I always seem to discover something I didn't realise I had – which is fun but also a little unnerving) and hate, hate, *hate* going through my kitchen cupboards (plastic containers seem to be breeding under my sink). So I take an afternoon and do them at the same time: the joy of sorting my books helps cancel out the pain of trying to get all those pots and pans to fit into the limited space of my kitchen cupboards.

However you decide to frame your sorting, you will need to use a grading system, which will force you to decide on each item's status. You should create three piles – one to throw out, one to sell or give away, and one to keep. Throw out those items which are really beyond repair and depress you – you know what they are (and just because someone has given you something doesn't mean you have to keep it, especially if you don't like it).

On another note (if you'll allow me a quick tangent), I think it is slightly intrusive to give people items to decorate their home if you don't really understand their style. The good intention is there, sure, but possibly not the thought. It's always much better to give presents that are not going to intrude on people's lives and homes – a CD, DVD, book, food, wine or even a gift voucher is much more practical and considerate than something they don't really like, which will clutter their home and become a dust-collector. It may not be as personal but ultimately it will be less pressure on both the giver and receiver. Unless you are really close to the person and know their taste, try not to give clothing or objects they haven't asked for.

Give away your surplus items to people who need them more than you, or sell them at a garage sale or on eBay. Make a day of it – take photos of all your items and then wait for the auction to begin. It can be fun selling your stuff, just don't get too caught up in the money you earn – you can get depressed thinking about what you paid in the first place. This is especially true if you have a stall at a flea market or a garage sale – people will haggle with you for a dollar here and there and it can be exhausting. Whichever way you decide, there are so many charity stores and recycling websites now, there is no excuse for not clearing your home of excess.

Assessing the value of each item is personal. I like to hold on to certain clothes that won't date, clothes that I think I will wear again even though they may not be in fashion at the moment. Professional organisers have rules about getting rid of clothes if you haven't worn them for six to twelve months, but again, my feeling is that this may not suit everyone. Decide for yourself whether you need to be strict or relaxed in your sorting. If you're likely to keep everything 'just in case', you might need to adopt a more rigid approach.

One of my favourite scenes in the *Sex and the City* movie is where Carrie tries on clothes from her past and her friends

vote on what she should keep and what she should cull. Those outfits represent moments and relationships in her life. If you are a sentimental soul like me, and can't bear to throw away your Anna Sui baby-doll dress because it reminds you of a time when you were queen of the dance floor, thin, naturally tanned, with no wrinkles or cellulite, then keep a suitcase or trunk where you store these treasures and get rid of the crap: the ripped, the stained, the broken, the gifts you never liked from people you never liked or from those who broke your heart.

All the items you have left in your 'Keep' pile are yours to enjoy. Wipe down the cupboards while they're clear and put these items back, in an organised way, so that they won't fall victim to more clutter in a matter of days. These are the things you've allowed yourself, so treat them well.

Don't pass on the habit

At the moment I don't have children, but my sister and friends do and they say that children's toys and paraphernalia quickly get out of control. So if you have kids, it might be a good idea to encourage de-cluttering habits sooner rather than later. Let them know that the toys they give away are going to children who are less fortunate than they are. It might be a bit of a shock initially, but you can get them used to feeling satisfied with fewer purchases – and you won't be creating mini over-shoppers. Kids seem to have a lot of toys these days but most of the time an experience will bring the most enjoyment. I know that my niece and nephew are most excited when I take them to the park for a good old-fashioned play or bake cookies with them (you'd be surprised how excited kids can get at sifting flour and breaking eggs).

Tips to remember

- Sort one room, cupboard or drawer at a time.

- Start sorting in the easiest place and move to the hardest – if your bathroom isn't too bad, start there. Then, you will slowly build your confidence and strength, and you will realise that you are capable of doing this.

- You need to entertain or distract yourself: put on your favourite music or set up your TV and play your favourite shows or movies (this is also helpful to ease the pain and boredom of doing your taxes or sorting out bills).

- Create three piles – one to throw out, one to sell or give away, and one to keep.

- Don't add to other people's stress and clutter when giving gifts. Ask them what they actually want or give them vouchers or something they consume – food, wine, CDs, DVDs or books.

- Keep things that mean something to you, but get rid of the crap – you know what it is.

Food Shopping

Market

- Broccoli
- Beans
- cherry tomatoes
- coriander
- rocket leaves
- asparagus
- Fish (600g)
- chicken fillets
- lamb cutlets

* Eggs (free range)

Deli

- Ricotta
- olives
- Ham shaved
- Dips
- Turkish bread

My Wishlist

> IPOD
> new couch
> new BBQ

New Winter Clothes

1. Boots
2. Jeans
3. Coat (rain)
4. Cocktail Dress 4 Party
5. Jumper
6. Work Dress

Christmas Presents

Mum — cookbook
Dad — web camera
Sally — Massage voucher
Vince — summer PJs
Jane — Kitchen scales
Nan — Teapot
Alice — Beach Towel
Sam — ABC Book
Lucy — choc Fondue Set

Chapter Four

*The boring stuff – build boundaries and learn
to play the shopping game*

I've done all sorts of crazy things when I've been stressed about a big event. I've run out and bought new cushions and rugs before a dinner party, which certainly didn't make my food taste any better or the man I was trying to impress find me any more attractive. I've gone straight from the airport to a Barney's warehouse sale, nervous about a big meeting and still dopey from a sleeping pill, only to walk out with a pair of pink furry Miu Miu slippers, orange Gucci slides and a purple coat (where on earth does one wear a purple coat?). And I once tried to find a formal outfit in New York, a couple of hours before the stores closed on New Year's Eve. I had seen a gold top in a magazine and was convinced that if I had that top I would look amazing and have a fabulous New Year (a night I'm always a bit angsty about). A friend who was visiting from Australia had arrived that day and, straight from the airport, I dragged her around half of Manhattan looking for this elusive gold top, which was going to change my life. Suffice to say it was a disaster: I lost my friend in Century 21 (the iconic discount designer store) among all the other crazy women trying to find the perfect outfit at 5 pm on New Year's Eve. I ended up having to get my friend paged on the loudspeaker system. She was in shock from the chaos, not to mention having her name called out in a department store a few hours after she'd landed in New York.

I never found that gold top, although I did buy a couple of things in the frenzy. When I got home and tried on the new outfits for my housemates (one was a fashion stylist, the other an actress), they told me I looked terrible, so I ended up wearing something I already had – not the first time this has happened and probably not the last. But I do try to avoid what I refer to as 'event shopping'.

That purchase that you think is going to change your life, ensure you have a wonderful night, make someone fall in love with you. These purchases are often made in a state of panic.

Before a formal event, when I know I will be tempted to buy something new, I now spend some time really going through my wardrobe to see if I can wear something I already have or a combination of things. I try to make this enjoyable by putting on upbeat music and I remind myself not to get too stressed. It is only one night – it's over in no time. Any credit card debt lingers much longer. Besides, at big events most people are worried about how they look themselves and often don't notice what other people are wearing. Think about the last wedding or big party you went to: you can probably remember what you wore but not what anyone else was wearing.

We tend to look and feel good about ourselves when we are fit and healthy (a fake spray-tan and a blow-wave can help too), but it's not all about the outfit, which is where I used to go wrong. Now I try to exercise and eat healthily before an event so that I feel better about myself, which I know will make me feel more confident – whatever I end up wearing.

The same goes for smaller events. When I entertain friends, I now spend more time planning the food I'm going to make

and the music I'm going to play, rather than trying to redecorate my home hours before my guests arrive. I think about who I am going to invite, what combinations of people will enjoy one another's company. I make it an event and enjoy the preparation of the evening, by taking out an old silverware set that my parents received for their wedding, using cloth napkins and working out where I would like people to sit. I have a few old CDs on standby, just in case the night gets late and some silly '80s music may be required. I'm embarrassed now to think I was running around buying rugs hours before people arrived for a dinner party, stressing myself out so much that by the time everyone arrived I was a wreck. Now my dinner parties are relaxed because *I* am; I make simple food and use the kooky dinner plates and glasses I've picked up at garage sales or been given, to add a personal touch. These days I find people just appreciate a home-cooked meal and spending some time in someone else's home, because we are all so busy and disconnected. Nights at a friend's house are generally more relaxed than those at a restaurant and it makes us appreciate values that we have lost touch with, old-fashioned values – home-cooking, good conversations – values that are not about instant gratification.

Patience, another of those old-fashioned values, is boring, but taking a step back and waiting before you purchase something is definitely worth it. If it's just a craving, it will pass. If you really, really need something, save up for it, like we used to – get a jar and put money in it from time to time. I remember saving up to buy my first record. My sister and I did odd jobs around the house and our parents gave us some pocket money each week in return. We kept the money in a jar and when it was almost full we were finally able to buy the soundtrack to *Grease*. I still remember how great it felt to achieve that goal; half the fun was in saving up for it. Part of it was just watching the coins slowly filling up the jar as we got closer to the top. I don't know about you, but I haven't felt this for a while – every time I look at my bank/credit card/ mortgage statements I don't seem to be moving very far forward. So bring the feeling back when you really need something. You'll appreciate it so much more if you've truly earned it.

It sounds obvious, but it's probably better to shop when you are happy and not rushed. Have you ever done last-minute shopping at Christmas time? You can feel the tension; people don't look happy, they look stressed. Subconsciously, or perhaps even consciously, they know they are getting themselves into debt by buying gifts their family and friends probably don't really need. The BBC did a poll a few years ago in which some people said they preferred a trip to the dentist to doing Christmas shopping. Other people interviewed said Christmas shopping was more stressful than looking after small children. And although many people enjoy receiving gifts (even the ugly ones), it's the purchasing that has pressure involved in it. Be carefree – go to the shops without pressure. Early mornings or late nights are calmer and help reduce the stress of being in crowds and lining up. In these quieter times the energy is relaxed and the fever less contagious. You're less likely to over-spend when you can think and consider your purchases. My sister does all her Christmas shopping in the middle of the year. She takes her time, makes lists and looks out for bargains. At Christmas time you generally don't have the luxury of doing this, especially if you leave it to the last minute, when you're bound to spend more than you planned.

You might never be as organised as my sister, but you can learn to play the shopping game. Plan your shopping, make lists – they work if you stick to them. Make both short-term and long-term shopping lists, so that you can actually save up for items that you need. If you need a new swimsuit for summer, start saving in winter or spring – work out how much it costs and how many weeks until you need it, and then you'll have the amount you need to put in the cookie jar each week. Deposit the money at the start of the week, so you won't be tempted to spend it on other things.

If you have ongoing lists of things you actually need, you can be more strategic about shopping – only going out when you have the money and then only visiting the specific store to make your planned purchase. I usually have a few ongoing lists. There's the weekly one, for food and essential items – I have all the usual things I need printed out and photocopied, so then I just highlight the item as I run out. It makes shopping easy and efficient. Then there are the longer term lists: items I will need for the next season – new winter boots, et cetera – and an aspirational items list for things like a new stereo, in case I get a windfall from somewhere.

A Stanford University study recently claimed that our brains gain pleasure not only from the things we buy, but also from the act of purchasing the product itself. Maybe it's the rush of anticipation of something new, or the flash and buzz of all the merchandise. So if you find you miss the act of shopping, allow yourself small treats. Go to a big discount store like Target or Kmart and give yourself a small budget. I used to have to do this; it got me through my darkest days. I would allow myself $20 and then spend a couple of hours walking around, finding things to buy. I'd usually end up with bubble bath and a book, or some socks or a magazine – this was before I had developed other hobbies and ways of dealing with my stress – but it would give me my fix and I would feel okay about it because I knew I hadn't gone into debt doing it. It sounds silly to all the sensible shoppers out there, but it makes sense to over-shoppers.

I also love doing this at garage sales and flea markets. I only take the cash I've budgeted for and that's it. I learned this from my mother. She's a great gourmet cook and she loves going to garage

sales looking for old cookbooks and kitchen bits and pieces. But she always sets herself a limit and she goes home when her budget is spent.

All of this is very individual. You need to try a few different things and figure out what works for you. Just remember to set yourself boundaries; you'll slowly adjust to them and build your own resolve. The more you resist the temptation to over-shop the stronger you will become and your over-shopping habit will have less control over you. It's like exercise – the more you do it, the stronger you get and the easier it feels. Over time you'll notice that you will be less likely to over-shop and more aware of your emotions when you feel the need to make those 'change your life' purchases. Soon you will be on the path back to conscious spending.

There is nothing wrong with spending money you have on things you really want, as long as you are fully aware and conscious about the purchase. It's when we're on emotional auto-pilot, handing over a credit card – in my case for yet another black top I don't really need – that we are not in the present moment and we're detached from our spending.

Tips to remember

- Wait.

- Build boundaries.

- Don't shop when everyone else is shopping –
  the frenetic energy is contagious.

- Do your Christmas shopping before everyone else,
  in July or August.

- Set your limits, go to an inexpensive department
  store, flea market, garage sale or discount store –
  you can shop within your budget and get your fix
  without feeling bad.

- If you have to shop, try to shop when you are
  happy.

- Create short-term and long-term lists – weekly lists
  for immediate essentials, and monthly and yearly
  lists for non-essential and big ticket items.

CREDIT CARD

1230 3204 7803 3040

05/05   04/11
MISS JANE STEVENS

THE BANK

SALE

0402 4557 9370 8533

VALID
FROM 06/08   UNTIL
END 04/12
MS MICHELLE K PETERS

Chapter Five

Sales are not your friend and
credit cards are the devil's work

Now this is my Michael Moore chapter. I need to tell you what I have discovered about credit cards – they are designed to take advantage of people like us. I was able to get my hands on some internal documents from a finance company that provides credit cards, and the way they perceive 'bad users of credit' is really disturbing. They call us 'The Impulsives'. According to the finance company, we 'find it difficult to budget', 'buy things on impulse' and 'will rarely or never pay off our credit cards'. The finance companies target us emotionally – apparently we feel financial pressure yet we still want to spoil ourselves and will therefore always use credit cards. So we continue to get increases on our credit cards and max them out, barely paying the minimum amount every month. Any advertising is pitched to appeal to the emotion of over-shopper needs – it's not about showing the function of the cards or how they work, it's purely emotive. The Impulsives keep credit card companies in business; that's why they target us and take advantage of us.

On the other hand, there are the 'Confident Planners', the 'wise users of credit' who plan their purchases and pay off their credit cards in full every month. They take advantage of the privileges that credit cards can provide without giving the companies any real benefits. They earn frequent flyer points, avoid paying annual fees or interest, and some even use credit cards to make money by using them to buy and trade shares. Credit card companies hate these people as they actually lose money on them. Lucky they have us suckers, The Impulsives, to take advantage of. The rest of us are paying ridiculous amounts of interest and late fees, so the credit companies continue to thrive and post record profits. Not unlike tobacco companies, they are evil.

Remember this next time you're tempted to whip out your credit card and make a purchase. I'm not a fan of cutting up credit cards – you do actually need one to exist in society these days, and travel is pretty much impossible without one, but you certainly don't need more than two so think about getting rid of some. When you pay with a credit card, you are also not as aware of the money you are spending. If you pay with cash, you will see the physical notes leaving your wallet, and you will feel it more.

I asked my father recently what they did before credit cards and he simply said, 'We saved our money and then bought what we needed.' It's a concept we seem to have lost sight of. We don't do the saving thing very much anymore – no delayed gratification for us! We eat fast food, we always have our phones with us, our emails are sent to our BlackBerries, we download TV shows from the Internet – all the waiting has been cut out of the equation. We want everything right away and we're always in a hurry. And it has become so easy to get everything now. You can watch *Next Top Model*, see a dress you like, go online and have the dress shipped to you with a few clicks. Think about the last time you were told that a store didn't have what you wanted in stock, but that they could order it in for you in two weeks. I bet you walked out, because you needed that fix immediately. Nothing worse for an over-shopper to come home empty-handed after a day out shopping – actually, I don't think it ever happens; we will buy because we want something *now*. Suddenly we're Veruca Salt from *Charlie and the Chocolate Factory*, screaming that we *want it now!*

Why do we want it now? Because speed is what our society worships, and slow is not cool. Advertising and marketing campaigns urge us to get out there and buy the new perfume/shampoo/car, otherwise we won't be complete. They play on our insecurities and we buy the message and rush out to buy the new shampoo so we can have bouncy hair and a new, improved life. We're so caught up in all this that we don't take the time to work out what's important and what we really need.

There is a little shop near me that sells antiques and collectibles. The elderly couple who run it have a long-term lay-by scheme, so you can put down a deposit and take a year to pay it off. It's very old-fashioned, but it celebrates earning something and really owning it, not just whacking it on a credit card and then selling it on eBay a few months later. We need to embrace the slow, considered purchase, in the same way that foodies have embraced the slow food movement. Slow it down, earn it and appreciate it, and don't get stung by the credit card companies.

As I write this, the world is facing a financial crisis and consumer credit card debt is at an all-time high. The best way to weather the storm, so the economists say, is to get out of debt. You can go online and find credit calculator sites, which figure out how long it will take you to pay off your credit card and how much items are costing you when you buy them on credit. Credit card interest rates generally range from 8 per cent to 20 per cent, and if you only pay the minimum amount each month, you are probably paying about 160 per cent of the item's original price. So, for example, that $220 handbag you want will actually cost you $352 on credit, once you account for the interest you're being charged. When you're in a shop, it's easier just to think of it as paying double.

These rates vary quite drastically and also depend on individual credit card fees, late fees and interest-free periods. And as shopping debt accrues and people have less cash on hand for essentials, they are using their credit cards to help pay for increasing food and fuel prices, making it harder to keep those cards under control. It's a bit like getting fat – it's easy and quick to put on weight, but it's hard to lose it. Once you have a high balance on your card it's really tough to get it down. There are heaps of books out there that give advice about reducing your debt, but if you are an over-shopper, you need to get your shopping under control first and then work out a plan to reduce your debts.

In June 2008, Australians were paying almost 12 per cent of their income on credit card interest – that's a lot of money for nothing! And credit cards are hard to cancel, especially charge cards. Like those terrible gyms that make you take an exit interview before you can leave, credit companies will make you jump hoops. You will need to make lots of calls and write letters – yes, actually write and send letters – it's not an easy system to get out of once you are in the credit cult.

Despite my intense dislike of credit card companies and their tactics, I have certainly been drawn in emotionally by them. I've had the same issue with loyalty programs, which I now bear a personal grudge against – they drive me mad and give me retail rage. If one more person asks me if I have FlyBuys, I will scream. The checkout people at my supermarket always ask me if I have this loyalty frequent shopping points scheme – some of them have served me for years and still ask. I need a badge that says, 'I don't belong to any loyalty clubs and if I wanted fries or a Coke with that I would have asked for it'. I have so many frequent flyer points from all my work travel, but I still can't seem to book a trip when I want, and, yes, people keep telling me it's supposed to be easier to book flights now, but in my experience when you want to travel during holiday times, it's near impossible.

If you can make loyalty programs work for you, then you are a better person than I am. All loyalty schemes and discount vouchers are designed to make you spend more money, usually in the same place, and they can be addictive – at one point I had so many loyalty cards in my wallet I could barely close it and I could never find the one I needed anyway. One of my friends was so obsessed with earning frequent flyer points to keep up her gold membership that she flew from Melbourne to Sydney for a day so as not to lose her status membership. And that's my issue: these schemes are designed to make you spend more money. If you are not an over-shopper, then you probably have the discipline to make them work for you, but if you're reading this book, chances are you should avoid them.

Plus, if you are using credit cards to earn these points, are you really earning them for free? Or are you chalking up more interest and late fees?

Beware the discount warehouse too – if these places work for you, great, but personally I find myself buying crap because it's cheap. *Hot pink cake stand? Leopard print slippers? Wallpaper I will never put up and two-for-one exercise DVDs I'll never watch? Bargains!* I know a lot of people love these stores, but if you're an over-shopper, going to a discount warehouse is like an alcoholic going to a cocktail party – it's best you stay away from them, rather than be led into temptation.

Sales are the same: you get caught up in the energy of it all and lose your common sense. If you have the ability to wait for a sale on a certain item, buy only the item you'd planned to buy (with cash) and walk out without buying anything else, then you can deal with sales. I can't do this. I invariably buy other stuff I wasn't intending to buy, and I usually put it on a credit card, which means that I am paying around twice as much as the sale price for something I didn't want in the first place. Not such a bargain when the sales haze lifts.

I don't know about you, but when I see a sale sign I become completely irrational – a tag saying 20 or 50 per cent off is enough to send me into a buying panic. *I couldn't possibly walk away from such a find – this might be the only opportunity I'll get!* Sales play on a last-chance mentality; it's like it's the end of the world and if you don't make that purchase right away, you will be missing out on something. You *won't* be missing out on something. Have you ever noticed how the really good stuff never actually goes on sale? It's the leftovers in odd sizes that make it to the sale racks. Better to save up and buy the great stuff, which you actually want, in the first place.

Duty-free stores at airports are also dangerous – there is already a certain amount of adrenalin and anticipation intrinsic to airports. You're about to hop on a plane, for an exciting holiday, an important business trip or a family reunion; you might be a nervous flyer or anxious about what lies in store for you at the end of the flight. Emotions are higher than usual. This in conjunction with discounted items – especially very attractive things, like expensive champagne, designer lipstick, cameras and iPods – means an over-shopper can blow their travel budget before they've even stepped on the plane. If you are able to buy your duty-free vodka and keep walking, then go ahead, but ultimately it is better to bypass duty-free altogether and go buy an interesting magazine to read on the plane instead.

So remember: sales are not your friend. If you are an over-shopper, you generally will not have the willpower or discipline when you see those enticing sale signs. If you buy an item on sale by putting it on a credit card, it's not a bargain; it will usually cost twice as much by the time you pay for interest and fees, if you're not paying your card off each month. So think like you would if you were in a foreign country: double the price to find out the real price. And only buy things on sale with your own money – that is, not with a credit card.

Tips to remember

- Avoid sales – it's too easy to get caught up in the frenzy and buy things you don't need.

- Avoid discount warehouses – you end up buying cheap crap.

- Loyalty cards and discount vouchers are more likely to take advantage of you than vice versa.

- Don't succumb to the 'last chance' mentality. You will usually get another chance to buy something.

- If you put it on a credit card it's going to cost you twice as much.

- Don't be one of the losers that credit card companies profit from. Become one of the Confident Planners, who profit from the companies instead.

Chapter Six

Sorry, but you can't actually shop your way to inner happiness

Okay, I'm going to get all spiritual and self-helpy here because, as you already know, shopping doesn't really – *not really* – make you happy. It can kill a bit of time or distract you, especially if you are a mother of small children, a stressed-out office worker or a bored student, but if shopping is attached to accruing debt then it is really just going to cause more stress in your life. You only need to turn on the news or a talk show to hear about the emotional stress

people are put under by debt; disagreements over money is one of the main reasons marriages break up. Financial stress seems to be everywhere, and we are watering the weeds by focusing on the issue of debt instead of focusing on the positive things in our lives and perhaps looking at how we can give back a little.

One of the things I've noticed about being stressed is that it can push you into corners where you make irrational decisions. I have a friend whose husband went off on a work trip while she was sick with two small children. She should have asked him to stay but she didn't, just as he should have offered to stay but didn't. So there was my friend, tired, sick and stressed out with her toddler and baby. She called me and said that she'd gone out and put a very expensive designer sofa on her credit card. She didn't know why she had done it and she was worried about what her husband would say when he returned from his trip. But as an outside observer I understood why – she wasn't getting the help she needed so she tried to make herself feel better, and for some reason a designer Italian sofa seemed the solution.

I found myself doing a similar thing on an overseas work trip where, as the only woman in the team, I felt insecure and alienated. I went out and bought an expensive pair of very high heels – indeed, they meant I was as tall as most of the men I was working with – but it didn't really help with the underlying issue of my feelings of inadequacy and loneliness. I realise now that I was trying to empower myself, which of course didn't work at all. Shopping, especially when you can't afford it, is not an empowering activity.

What I have found works is to think about the things that make you happy. It's a lot easier to jump in your car and go to the shopping mall than it is to take time to learn a new skill or hobby, but it's less gratifying too. Learning golf for the past few years has taught me patience and an earned sense of achievement, even though I am still quite terrible at the actual sport. I usually embarrass myself, but I don't take it too seriously and I get to gossip with my friends when I play, much to the dismay of the serious male golfers on the course. (Want to see sexism at play? Visit a golf course – the last bastion of male superiority.) Still, it's been fun to infiltrate that world and not let myself be intimidated – moving out of your comfort zone and trying new challenges can be an antidote to over-shopping as it builds your confidence.

It might take a while to remember what does make you happy, though. When shopping has been your emotional crutch for so long, the other good things might have faded in significance. So take the time to remind yourself. I'm a listmaker from way back, so one thing that seems to help me is writing a list of all the things that usually make me feel better. I keep it in my wallet so it's easy to access, because when you are stressed or feeling down it's hard to think of these things. My list is simple and includes some daggy things: call a friend for a chat; have an ice-cream; take a bubble bath; have a nap or meditate; watch an episode of a favourite sitcom; get a pedicure; buy some organic fruit; walk along the beach; go to the driving range; see a movie; bake some cookies; make some soup; dance; read some poetry; look through some old *Oprah/Vanity Fair/New Yorker* magazines; eat a chicken pie; write in my journal; read a play aloud; do some yoga; think about someone I love; go for a swim; read a book at the beach – and the list goes on. Write your own list and put it somewhere you can refer to. It sounds silly and you probably think my list is dorky, but it does really help. Sometimes I feel better just reading my list as it contains all the things I like doing, which I often forget about doing. And if all else fails I try to do something nice for someone else, and that always makes me feel better.

Whenever I'm having a bad day, I try to turn it around by thinking of something I could do to make someone feel better. I do something small like call my grandmother, who lives alone and is always happy to hear from me. Or my parents, who live in another city and enjoy hearing about what I've been doing. Sometimes I'll donate a small amount of money to a charity online, or go into the city and give a homeless person a larger amount of money than they are used to receiving, say, $20. They are always so shocked, sometimes they will even ask if you're sure they can have it – that always gives me a buzz. I discovered this by accident, when a friend told me to donate the money I was trying to give her in return for a favour. At the time I was living in the city, so it was actually easier just to hand it to someone who looked like they needed it, rather than give it to an organised charity. I gave the money to a homeless woman and she was so thrilled, and it made me so happy, that now I do it from time to time.

These are the things that can give you longer lasting happiness. You just have to remember what makes you happy outside of shopping, and then do them.

But the thing is, you can't expect to be happy all the time. We all have sad days, stressful days and happy days – that's life. It seems that for some reason there is pressure for us to be 'up' all the time, and that's impossible. We need the rain to appreciate the sun,

and the dark to appreciate the light – it's not being particularly philosophical, it's really just how it is. I know so many people on antidepressants these days, it's incredible. Some of them truly need them to function, but I think others just need to feel good all the time. Sadness is okay – it teaches us about ourselves and it's a necessary part of growth. Sit with it for a bit; it's not that bad to be blue from time to time, and we become more aware of who we are.

The simple truth is that over-shopping will not make you happy, and having more money probably won't make you happy either. A big f-off TV is not as enjoyable to watch if whenever you turn it on you're reminded that you're paying 18 per cent interest on the repayments. I've certainly bought some dumb things for the wrong reasons, to impress someone or because I felt like it would change my life, but they never do – a new portable airconditioner didn't make the job I disliked any better and a man never asked me out because he liked my shoes – well, not a straight man anyway. What would make me happy is being debt-free. *That* will give you peace of mind, which is a pretty good feeling.

One of my friends told me that she and her husband couldn't afford to have a baby because they had too much credit card debt.

They had been one of those couples who always had great overseas holidays and went out for dinner to expensive restaurants, and bought lots of status-symbol items – a sports car, Italian designer furniture, a high-end stereo, a very big TV and works of art. Then in their mid-thirties they found themselves with a lot of stuff but still renting, without the home or family they hoped to have.

Don't let your over-shopping stop you from doing the things you really want to do. Think about spending your money on experiences, like learning a new skill or sport, or travelling somewhere new, instead of always buying things.

Being wealthy is not worrying about money. Having a cupboard full of fashionable clothes is not going to give you any comfort when you wake up in the middle of the night with a panic attack about the amount of money you owe on your credit cards. It also won't give you comfort about the things that frustrate you in your life – job/husband/parents/kids/boyfriend/teacher. And those shoes and clothes – no matter how lovely – will definitely not make you feel great when you get those bills and collection notices in the mail. I went through a stage when I just didn't want to open my letterbox, especially after a bad day at work, because I knew I would just be more depressed once I opened the latest bills.

Learning to appreciate again can also really help. Any gifts you receive will feel different. You could give your family and friends a list of a few things you would really like for your birthday or Christmas – it will be helpful to them and it means that you will receive gifts that you want or need. When you don't over-shop, gifts from other people are a real treat. My mother gave me a beautiful rose quartz elephant to sit on my desk while I write as a good luck charm; when I look at it I smile. It gives me inspiration and I hold it when I'm stuck for words. It's a gift with sentiment – if I had bought it for myself with a credit card I can't imagine it would mean that much to me.

Learn to express yourself without shopping – keep trying new things. And be grateful for what you already have – it's already a great deal more than many people will ever have.

Tip to remember

- Write a list of twenty things you enjoy doing – things that make you happy – and carry it with you in your wallet. Refer to it when you are stressed, bored or sad. And especially when you feel like going out and spending lots of money you don't have.

Chapter Seven

*Okay, here it is – the journey back
to conscious spending*

At some point you need to consciously let go of your over-shopping.
I've been meditating for years and have found this really helps me
centre my thoughts. When I was trying to get control of my over-
shopping I would end my meditation sessions by thinking of my
over-shopping (and my credit card debt) as a bunch of balloons,
then I would imagine myself letting them go and watching them
float away into the sky. It's a gentle way of releasing something

that is negative in your life, including situations or people or even decisions you're not sure about – let it all go. It might seem a bit new-agey or spiritual for you, but think of ways you can let go of your shopping. I know a businessman who, when he has a bad day, rips it out of his desk calendar and burns it. This seems a little extreme to me but it's more about moving on, and the next day being a new start.

In the UK recently the media reported that a third of all food bought was thrown out and 40 per cent of that was made up of fruit and vegetables. This has a huge impact on the environment as rotting food produces greenhouse gases, not to mention all the energy required to grow, harvest and transport the food. If we just bought the food we needed, the environment would be better off and we'd all save money. There are communities of people called Freegans, who exist by what they call 'urban foraging' and 'dumpster diving'; that is, they live off what other people discard. It may sound an unattractive option to most people, but it does illustrate how wasteful our society has become. As a survivor of a world war and a depression, my grandmother never wastes food and as a child I was always amazed at her ability to create a meal from nothing. To this day she cannot bear to throw food out. We could live and consume more responsibly if we looked at how our grandparents lived or how some of these alternative communities manage to survive.

My street recently had a council hard-rubbish collection and the items people put on the street were astounding – sofas, surfboards, kids' bicycles, half-dead plants and exercise equipment bought with good intentions. When you see the level of consumption and clutter around, it's not surprising that some people are saying no to consuming altogether. When you try to cut down on your own shopping, it might be helpful to see how some people have chosen to exist. Most religions espouse fasting or abstinence at certain times – it's always been seen that some 'giving up' is good for the soul – from Catholics who give up something at Lent, to Jews who fast at Yom Kippur and Muslims who fast at Ramadan.

In the late 1990s I heard the American writer Douglas Rushkoff give a lecture in Melbourne. He spoke about the notion of not spending on one day of the week, in the Judeo-Christian tradition, which is millions of years old. You don't have to subscribe to religion to take this on board. It's a day of rest, for both you and your wallet. It certainly had quite an impact on me and I used to try it every now and then. It takes some planning, but having a

day when you don't actually hand over any money feels strangely liberating – it's hard to leave the house without using money these days, but try to see if you can do it as part of your shopping detox. You'll start to see the things you can do that cost nothing.

I'm also a big fan of the pyjama day. When I was living in New York I sent my mother a cartoon by Victoria Roberts from *The New Yorker*. It had a woman in pyjamas talking to her husband, who was looking curiously at her while she announced, 'I'm having a pyjama day,' like it was a very normal thing to do. It has now become a running joke in my family. Even my five-year-old niece requests a pyjama day every now and then. Basically, it's a day to stay at home in your pyjamas and potter around – eat, read, watch TV, nap, take baths. You don't have to be anywhere or do anything important, you don't have to wash your hair or wear make-up, you can just 'chillax'. I encourage you to try one every now and then.

If you *are* going to shop, see if you can create some good karma for yourself by buying eco-friendly products, items from charity stores, fair-trade coffee and tea, organic cotton, even conflict-free diamonds. Or you can be supportive of your local farmers by buying food at a grower's market or shop at your local butcher, grocer, convenience store – sometimes it's just good to support the little guy. It's still shopping, but it's a more conscious form of it. You're not just switching off and going automatically into stores. I like to shop at my local stores despite the fact that the items may be a little more expensive – I find that I spend less than when I go to a large supermarket, where I am enticed by two-for-one offers and items on sale. But mainly I enjoy engaging with my local community, and giving back.

Another way to give back is to literally give away – charities that used to rely on donations say that they have a lack of furniture, household items and clothes to provide to the needy, because many people tend to have garage sales now, rather than donate items. Why not have a garage sale and donate half the money you make to a charity? Or find a charity that will come and pick items up? My sister and I found a lovely old couple who were spending their retirement picking up household items for African refugees. They mentioned that there were many children who were in need of school items, so I donated a desk and a lamp with stationery supplies – it was good to feel like I was helping someone in need. Go online to research charities so you can contribute to something that has meaning for you.

If you feel like you need to get on top of your own debts first, then look to places like eBay to sell your surplus items, especially before you make new purchases – keep the energy in your home flowing by having things leave before you let new things enter your life. It will also help avoid clutter building up, which you have probably experienced as an over-shopper. Think about the movie *27 Dresses*, in which the main character keeps twenty-seven bridesmaid dresses, holding onto the past and letting it hold her back. I don't know about you, but I felt relieved when she finally stuffed them into garbage bags, because now she will be able to move on and live a fuller life (and of course fall in love and live happily ever after). It's just a movie, I know, but the symbolism of it is strong for us over-shoppers, and on some level we can all relate to it. Shift your clutter and start a more authentic life.

Once you do get your over-shopping and credit card debt under control, you might want to consider spending your money in areas that will actually enhance your life. Instead of buying stuff, spend it on services – a cleaner, a personal trainer or learning a new skill. Even going to have a massage, which will reduce stress and is good for your health, is cheaper than making an extravagant purchase. Years ago I realised I could afford a cleaner to come to my house once every two weeks for two hours instead of buying my breakfast on the way to work every morning. By giving up my

No Shopping Day

coffee and muffin I got a clean home in return – now that was a great investment. Think about how you can shuffle your money around to spend it on things that will truly make a difference: learning to cook new food, dancing, taking a creative writing class – make your own list.

It's also time to start thinking about giving some money away. You're probably not as badly off as you think you are, and as you reduce your credit card debt it would be a great thing to think about sponsoring an under-privileged child or other charity. In many countries charity donations are tax deductible,

so there really is a great incentive and not much of an excuse not to. However, if giving money is not possible for you yet, what about giving some of your time? Even a couple of hours once a month can make a difference and it will really make you feel good, and grateful for what you have. A few years ago I volunteered at a charity warehouse which supplies clothes and food to various different charities. One of the things I was sorting was baby clothes, something in very short supply. It was quite an eye-opener and it made me a little teary to realise some people couldn't afford to dress their babies. I also spent time handing out food supplies to people and, again, it made me realise how lucky I was and how much I needed to appreciate my life. Somehow it puts your shopping cravings into perspective.

Tips to remember

- Give away what you don't need or use; you will be helping someone and liberating space in your home.

- Have a garage sale or stall at a market, or sell things on eBay.

- Have a bank account (or jar) where you keep the money from your sales and then use this as your shopping money or emergency funds, or to pay off credit cards.

- If you still have the receipt for something you haven't used yet, see if you can return it.

- Spend money on things that will improve your life – get a cleaner or personal trainer, have a massage, learn a new skill.

- Donate some money or your time to help people less privileged than yourself – it will make you feel great and grateful for what you already have.

Conclusion

What does not kill us makes us stronger –
or so they say …

This is the part of the book where I wrap it all up and give you my last pearls of wisdom, but as I write this final chapter, my spirit is somewhere else. But I'll get back to that.

This is what I was going to tell you: don't be a victim of finance and credit card companies. Whenever you think you are going to buy something, think about whether it will really change your life, then think about the real cost – if you are putting it on a credit card you are not going to pay off straight away, you are probably going to end up paying double for it.

Spend time discovering new things to do besides shopping, and rediscover a hobby you enjoyed when you were younger. Remember instant gratification is usually not as rewarding as the things that take time and effort to achieve.

And yes, it will be hard and you will feel crap at times, and you will have moments when you will fall off the over-shopping wagon. But you will get through this and be stronger for it.

Once you have got your over-shopping under control and feel like you have truly made the journey back to conscious spending, then you can start reading all those finance and money books out there that advise you on how to get your finances in order. And if you actually have money you don't know what to do with, you should think about giving some of it away, or go consult a financial planner – just watch out for those ones that tell you to give up your sponsor children and stay at home and eat eggs! I did end up finding one that wasn't *quite* so bad …

The really nice financial planner who broke my heart, but made me understand what was important
While I was working on the second draft of this book, I met a

financial planner socially and told him about my book and the experiences I had had. He told me to come in and we would discuss my financial situation so he could prove that all financial planners were not the same. Again, I was embarrassed at my situation, but he was a nice man and he said that he could help me get back on track. By this time, I had stopped my over-shopping, but I'd had a couple of years of emergency situations which I had no savings to cover – car repair work, surgery and dental work – all necessary and all paid for with credit cards that were already bursting at the seams from my over-shopping days.

The nice financial planner suggested I sell my apartment, pay off all my debts and start again. He said I could rent for a few years and save money, without changing my lifestyle too much, as I was on a good salary. It made sense financially. He suggested I could eventually look into buying property once I was in a secure place, because I needed to consider my retirement as I was not going to receive an inheritance and, yes, still no husband to share that damn mortgage with. The visions of becoming a Jane Austen spinster who lived with her geriatric parents were returning.

I went home and cried that night because I realised that the sense of belonging I had in my apartment was what was important, not what was in it – duh. Anyway, I like this financial planner but I'm not going to sell my apartment, because in the words of Dorothy, 'There's no place like home,' and somehow I am going to keep mine, even if I have sell everything in it. So the nice financial planner and I are going to work out a plan B. Now that I have my over-shopping under control I need to create a safety net for those curve balls that life throws, and as I get older they seem to be coming at a faster rate.

* * *

Now I feel I need to share something else with you as you've been on this journey with me. Three days ago I was diagnosed with breast cancer – it's such a cliché that I am almost embarrassed to talk about it. I'd just turned forty and I had decided that I would not have an existential crisis like I did on most birthdays, because what was the point? My life seemed to be on track – after years of meandering I felt like I knew where I was going, where I wanted to be and the sort of people I wanted to be part of my life. But the universe, it seemed, had other plans for me.

And so here I am, my life changing in an instant and making me realise what's really important, just in case I still hadn't got it. I thought writing this book would be enough to heal me of my over-shopping, and it has, but now I see that this illness is here to ensure I never forget what matters.

All those clichés about health are true, but that's not to say you can't still look good while you are feeling crap. I still wore my favourite sunglasses, skirt and shoes (which I had saved up to buy) as a friend drove me to hospital to receive the diagnosis.

So my dear over-shoppers, look after yourselves, be happy, become conscious spenders, work out what is really important to you. And don't let the credit card monsters bite.

Love, health and happy conscious shopping,
Neradine xxx

Acknowledgements

To my sister, Victoria, and with immense gratitude to the rest of my family for their love and support – Mum, Dad, Baka, Scotty, Mads and Max.

And to the friends who gave me advice on the book – Lizzie, Sophie, Mark, Limor, Gretel and Miriam.

And thanks to my editor, Emma, who listened to my pitch in the first place.